*Finding
Your Courage*

HIGH NOTES *of* POETRY

ELLEN BROWN HARRISON

PALMETTO
PUBLISHING
Charleston, SC
www.PalmettoPublishing.com

Hardcover ISBN: 979-8-8229-4480-0
Paperback ISBN: 979-8-8229-4481-7
eBook ISBN: 979-8-8229-4482-4

HIGH NOTES *of* POETRY

ELLEN BROWN HARRISON

CONTENTS

High Notes of poetry is dedicated to Willie "Bill" Brown

COURAGE

As our world is filled with sickness and death, it's also filled with riches and health. As the waves push toward the earth's shore and the sun rises as the world brightens, unfolding before us, behind us, and around us, it's symbolic of God's horizon. The stars twinkle in darkness for the world to shine; to push, to rise, to shine through adversity—that's courage, that's mine.

Through your mind and your spirit you seek courage, the courage that makes you a conqueror, the courage that makes you stronger, and the courage that makes you bolder. Through your heart you hold on to that courage, that moment in time when you are no longer defeated, no longer mistreated.

That courage is taking you to your next level of *Yes, I will,* with all in me I am going to be fulfilled. That courage is going to make me say, *Yes, I can*; for the future I hold in my hand. That courage will even make me say, *No* to that strong hold, when I refuse to be no longer controlled.

Let your new growth of courage be free to the world as the world is your pearl, building one strand at a time; live your life as it was ordainly divined.

CONFIDENCE

No longer being silent from within, we transcend from being shut up inside and unfolding our world to be open, and we see it quiet wonderfully. You see its self-reliance, self-assurance, owning our moment masterfully. We look at ourselves and see greatness and stand with straightness. We prepare our mind, body, and soul for excellence.

We speak excellence into existence, because we are magnificence. When you are magnificent, you don't concern yourself with being insignificant; you concern yourself with being different with your uniqueness.

We know who we are; we see our inner mystery. We accept who we are, and revel in it. We consent to every experience near and far, owning our confidence.

A CONFIDENT WOMAN

Intrigued by her entrance, all eyes in the room are captivated by her presence. She exudes confidence, resiliency; she has an aura that pulls people in, the energy that wins. It's her depth, her self-efficacy; she has no limits, but watches her steps—you best believe there are no missteps. She knows her weaknesses and owns her strength; there are no limits to her length. She is her own light, influential, intellectual, a woman in her own right.

She owns her physique; they wonder why she is so unique. She's a mystery, she's that puzzle to figure out piece by piece. She's like the queen of the chessboard, the most powerful, the one that scores, her moves can't be limited—the game would diminish—through her it's the only way to finish.

It's her resilience, she's brilliant, she will figure out how to overcome difficulties. She's courageous with her values, empowering on her beliefs and matters. She won't be minimized in order for you to be magnetized; she knows how to endure because she's secure. She believes we all can achieve in our lives—hey, she's the person that births life.

Labels and logos she can wear, but they don't matter; she brings her own style and flare.

Her beauty lies within, beyond any measure, like a beautiful golden star to treasure. Her charm and grace enlighten any face, with a warm seraphic embrace; she fascinates with her glow, unshakable in her flow, she moves with confidence, don't you know, she's a confident woman! A confident woman—that's her, a confident woman—that's you, a confident woman—that's me!

A CONFIDENT MAN

He displays the gentleman-like qualities of kindness, a distinctive sense of gentleman-like-mindedness, as he doesn't try to control the one he holds. He is of courage and of vigor with resilient strength of body and mind as he sees himself in the mirror. The respect and the value he has of other opinions, as he tunes in and learns from all genders. His intellect cultivates his thoughts, captivates, with his abilities to create and innovate. He is of great strength as he glides in with a sauntering walk; he engages every eye with smile and a brief talk.

He trusts his instincts, he looks distinct, and he leads with intent with his acquaintances. He has a vision, makes his own decisions, and is not afraid of the opposition. He pursues with purpose, passion, and determination; he's his own motivation. His individuality is essential, but he surrounds himself with positive force to help him reach his potential.

He treats every person with the utmost respect; he doesn't neglect, he protects; and with grace he handles conflict. A mindset of a confident man will not waver. He's assertive but precise, and he always has a plan and prevails. He has a positive demeanor, making the best out of every situation, moves forward without any hesitation. He helps to empower others, without feeling so powerful as to belittle others.

He's eloquent; the smell of his cologne is of just the right scent. He has a sense of style that is dignified. He's physically fit with a comical wit. He articulates fluently, coherently—a man of this stature is the most trustworthy. He loves in the right way, he does not stray, and he gives his lover deep affection day by day. He brings forth warmth and comfort; it's no effort when he holds his love in his arms, fulfilling his love with compassion, devotion, and charm. He's a confident man—that's he, a confident man—that's him, a confident man—that's them, a confident man—that's you.

THE STRENGTH TO RISE

Often you are beat down by society, and it's hard to find the strength to rise. The sound of the alarm in the morning is the most annoying noise in the world; it makes you want to pull them covers up and submerge. Submerge back into a fantasy and not face reality.

Sometimes you just can't get out of bed with all the noise in your head. A lot of times you are so weak from life's adversities you do not know what's ahead. The death of a loved one is making you weak, the loss of a job leaving you bleak, the end of a relationship, losing friendship, dealing with addictions, being overweight, underweight, ill. I know there are times when you are just run down, overwhelmed, fed up, tired, exhausted, full of anxiety and worn out about life. How can you find my strength to rise when life just keeps making me fall? How can you stand tall? All these factors make us lose momentum, but in times like these, find your strength to overcome them.

Seek help, no more time to mope! Are you going to rise from this, or is this it? Don't think there is no hope!

What do you choose? Choose not to lose. Choose yourself I say rise and continue to rise. It's an everyday occasion to rise from the adversities of life and to find your stride, find what makes you tick or click. Find your strength to rise, and don't let your life be demised.

Be fueled by your strength to rise—that means you get another chance for interventions, creativity, laughter, love, happiness. Remember we are God's partners in this world. When you choose God you are his partner, this is for every boy and girl! So don't be surprised when a birth of an idea comes to you to rise and make a difference. He trusts you to carry through what he has given you. Let your strength rise to your truth; bring forth new opportunities, new gifts, new desires, new growth changes, and new abilities to help others.

Just take a moment and close your eyes and let your imagination take you to another place. Let your imagination give you hope and see yourself rising to stand for the future you hold in your hand. Be joyful in hope, patient in affliction, faithful in prayer from your heart that you will have strength to rise to your truth. We may fall nine times, but we stand up at ten; that's how we win! It is possible that as one thing in life wanes, another thing rises to the forefront and you may discover a whole new meaning to life. That is what we call life. This is what we call true life living and not just existing!

TURN TEMPORARY INTO EVERLASTING

Temporary moments are fun; they give you high moments, the feeling ebullient. The use of drugs gives you that temporary high feeling, which leads to self-destruction and drinking alcohol to the maximum consumption. Oftentimes we stay on the run, fulfilling these temporary satisfactions, not meeting daily obligations, still feeling full of emptiness. These little temporary moments are not helpful for your sanity; you still are empty when you come back to reality.

Through chasing your temporary moments, search for your everlasting moments. That's your gift, that natural ability that gives you capability to inspire to lift. For every moment in time where you have listened and paid attention, for every moment in time when you have observed and learned, for every moment in time when you have read and comprehended, those are the everlasting moments that capture every essence of your being, that help you find your true meaning.

Be fueled by these moments. These moments are what help you find your gift of creativity, so don't be surprised when you birth that idea that comes to help you rise to your destiny. You are trusted to carry and bring forth the gift, the gift that brings new opportunities, new abilities, understanding that is everlasting.

PERSEVERE

You display a look of uncertainty, that absurdity! Why the look of self-doubt on your face? Is there a reason for this dismay? No need to doubt when you pray. Persevere through your lack of confidence and persevere to find your self-worth. Persevere through the points of feeling low, but persevere to the place that helps you grow. Persevere to make your dreams a reality using your essence of creativity and knowledge to reach your highest achievements.

Persevere through the difficulties and the lack of opportunities, persevere to resolve the difficulty and find the solutions! Stay steadfast and break through the walls that continue to fall. Everything that falls is not meant to stay down. Persevere to rise and find your crown!

Persevere for the life you deserve and don't let your dreams fade away; those dreams are to be achieved one day. You can achieve if you believe. As long as you are here in the atmosphere, you must persevere!

PURSUE

Wake up! Wake up! You can't keep dreaming and do you think like is easier that way when you are not achieving! That's an outrage! Don't let the fear of reality keep you in doubt, or you will always be left out! Life is full of obstacles, and it seems like the problems around us are astronomical, but they are solvable.

You must arise from that inferior state of mind and come into existence and make your world shine. There is brightness in this world that overcomes darkness; there are shadows that must stay behind in order to reach your greatness. The world is not perfect, but it's full of beautiful views if you pursue the wondrous feeling of fulfillment and accomplishments, It's the magnificence feeling of mastering and conquering.

The pursuit of success is not measured by your money, fame, or address, but by your happiness. Find your joy, shout it with ahoy! That's the ultimate meaning of pursuit, to find your happiness and bring forth the goals inside of you and to make a difference in what you do when you pursue.

TRUTH DEFINED

Our authenticities, are we allowing them to be dismissed? Do you know what your truth is?

To dismiss your truth and let it drift from your essential nature, not to nurture it to the surface is danger; why not let your truth become your game changer!

Often times we make decisions by the entertainment of television and not by our own vision or have become what other people have decided for us and then later ask the question: Do I know who I am? Am I not examining myself to figure out my own program? How am I going to pass this life exam when I don't know who I am?

Listen to your inner self to know what type of person you want to be or the person you don't want to be; nobody knows you better than yourself, can't you see?

Daily you have heard and were taught a lot of lessons and received advice from all types of sources; those lessons shared with you had to be deciphered and resonated for you to make life choices.

It does not matter how late in life you begin to find out what makes you who you are; it's what you do with your truth that makes you the victor.

Sometimes we find our truth through hurt and pain; when you are at your lowest point, you have to come to the realization to let the strength of your truth rise and bring you a float. Your truth is where you start swimming and cannot be dimmed; it helps you to take one stroke at a time, revealing your purpose and passion that makes you well defined.

Your "truth" is your freedom, and that's your newfound stardom. The statement the "truth" will set you free is for you to process into that which you were called to be.

DIMENSIONS

We have many dimensions of life, some are with losses, struggles, and defeats, through prayer and grace will lead to your triumphs and victory!

We have to tell ourselves it's a new day a new revelation that I am stepping into not fearing any of the devils.

Some of the steps will be small, some will be in the middle, and some will be large; no matter how many steps; take them with charge. Some will want to measure you by your past, limit and label you to finish last. Whether you finish first or last, the race is not giving to the swift lean on your own proportion of depth; stay steadfast and rise in breadth.

Let your range of truth extend far and beyond any dimension, with the least apprehension, so no one will have the least comprehension of how you reach your highest potential. This is not going to be easy, but it leads you to a statue of liberty, a place of freedom, knowing you are not going to be limited to bondage, opposition that blocks your steps in reaching your highest dimension.

THE DON'T-FIT-INS

You don't fit in and that's okay. You are not to people please and try to accommodate. The don't-fit-ins are more self-sufficient; they don't have a need for attention. They don't conform and have no interest to be part of the norm. They are outside-of-the-box doers and define their own way; they are not easily persuaded, and not easily intimidated! They are keen and not copiers and manage their way through any situation. They take risks and have willingness to venture out, because they are not bound to accompany the crowd.

One hopes you would treat a person like you want to be treated no matter what the circumstances may be; everybody bleeds the same blood underneath whether it's he, she, or me. Everyone deserves to be treated with the utmost respect in all situations; remember at the end of the day we are all God's creations.

Stop the bullying and let the don't-fit-ins roam to be free; they are setting a new standard of true equality. Embracing everyone's differences and releasing the dimness allows everyone to shine in their own uniqueness. No one deserves to live in fear, as everyone wants to live fiercely and become the next great pioneer. So don't worry about fitting in; be confident knowing you love yourself from within.

INEQUALITY

The world is experiencing the second revolution of inequality, and this is through our justice system. Protests are happening throughout this country; many innocent people become the victims.

Black and white Americans have taken to the highways, social media, and the major news outlets to get the message out loud and clear: we have to have equality in our justice system to help end racism.

The year 2020 was the year of enough; people had time to reflect on stuff. It was year of the perfect vision, and America is demanding fair decisions in our judicial system. We are declaring change, working for change, demanding change and becoming the change. We are saying their names, with a message that their deaths were not in vain.

We have experienced a rise of taking to the streets to protest; to grow and fight for progress, and we did not digress. It's now the time of coming to the forefront and as uncomfortable and hurtful as it was to watch another innocent person get killed, we stand united, law abiding, raising our voice, fighting for the cause! Fighting the justice system to rewrite the laws for equality, to help end inequality!

QUIET RACISM

This form of racism is through quiet words, which are heard but are overlooked—but left you a little shook! Did they just say that? But you are startled and think it's just an act.

The antagonism one can experience with quiet racism, when one is thinking they are superior, leaving the one experiencing the racism inferior. Inferior to make believe they are of low quality, to experience all kinds of inequality with this type of mediocrity!

This racism that goes on where everyone is not paid fair, when you are not hired for a job because of your skin color or the way you style your hair. When you get the sly remarks, oh you know how those types are; these remarks are going too far. Quiet racism is that form of racism where a person cannot be typically be punished, because it requires a whole lot of evidence and it's often diminished.

In order for quiet racism to be exposed, let the truth be known, speak with confidence, and be prepared to provide your evidence.

Quiet racism is another form of bondage when you don't speak up. Allowing ourselves to be completely free, not allowing a person to make remarks about your identity.

Stereotyping plays a part that formulates the path of racism; often based on misconceptions and incomplete information, harmful as it portrays false generalizations.

Be wary of the language used and topics discussed and the terms like they and us; making derogatory comments about a particular element of a person's culture or customs. A person can't help where they are from, but everyone deserves a chance to know who they will become. Speak out on unfair criticism to bring a light to quiet racism.

KNOCKING

We're knocking, we're knocking, but we are not completely in.— could it be the language we speak, or the color of our skin? Dr. King had a dream to put this kind of act to an end. They say we have overcome, but why we still feel so numb as our feelings are often dismiss, but this poem is written to continue with awareness that all race are not equally accepted and continue to be neglected. They say we should be grateful that we are partially accepted, but yet we are still so neglected, because of injustice and poverty.

With the knocking it's now time to open the doors and break down the barriers and stand up for important factors like fairness with pay, quality health care, and education matters!

We all have dreams like Dr. King did, so we're going to continue to push, no longer being silent and stop dealing with unfairness as this type of act should be ancient! It's not in the past and this can't continue to last. We are going to keep a smile on these pretty faces and fight for our race; as Dr. King would want us to do, because god's grace is not given to swiftness, but one that endures.

WATCHFUL

Pay attention to the look that people use to read you like a book; it's a stare in their glare; that you need to be aware. It's that look up and down with their face frown, the un-comfortableness in their body language as they look at you in anguish.

It's the demeanor of their nosiness that you notice from their entrance. The peripheral vision catches it all as they come to your presence. Your intuition will let you know that people's feelings are not easy to hide when they give you that look from the side not knowing you have that watchful eye.

FORGIVE

Stop feeling angry or resentful toward someone for their offense, flaw, or mistake; that's nonsense! Stop giving that person all your power and carrying all that dead weight, for heaven's sake! When you rise above and find the power to forgive, then you are letting go and will really start to live.

Forgiveness sets you free and gives you oxygen; it gives you freedom to release all the negative toxins.

Not forgiving weighs you down and causes all kinds of unwanted stress; it gives that person power over you that leaves you lifeless.

Not forgiving makes you weak, complex, leaving you feeling vexed. When you give that person so much power over you, you don't see your value. Do you want that person to have all of your strength by not forgiving? I think not. Once you allow a person to take your strength, you allowed that person to take your ability to live freely, losing yourself completely. Only you can give yourself the freedom of forgiving and truly start living!

To be set free is to forgive, to be free is to forgive, to live free is to forgive, and it starts with you to just forgive.

POSITIVITY

Positivity builds strength, yet it's very difficult most times to be positive. We don't always want to be positive with what is going on in the world daily often can lead you down a road of negativity. How can we be positive with all these random shootings in the air, leaving families with loss and despair! How can we be positive about viral sickness, experiencing all this weakness? How can we be positive when our children are not well, experiencing all this hell? How can we be positive when we think we are not beautiful, when we are excluded? How can we be positive when we are not enough, when life gets tough?

These negative thoughts will wear you down and leave you aground! We as humans tend to focus on the negative, but we need to find a way to release these types of thoughts and move toward positive thoughts. Remember—positive outweighs the negative every time; remember the number line? Speak positive affirmations and declarations, give yourself that motivation and watch your transformation of determination that leaves you in a triumphant jubilation!

A positive balance leaves you in an overflow; you have room to grow! Tell yourself you are enough, giving you the confidence to strut your stuff! Every day I am getting healthier, and every day I am living better! I am going to be joyful; because I am thankful! I am love because of the God above!

STRENGTH IN TEARS

Through negative and joyful aspects of life we shed a tear. Tears can do wonders for our emotions; they cleanse our soul and help us become unbroken. Whether the tears are for happiness or sadness, they help facilitate social bonding and help us see clearer. The value of tears is more of the social response. When you receive support, they become less intense and more of a rapport.

Tears do much more than just moisten and protect our eyes; they are a relief we need during distress and happy times. Please don't think tears make us feel weak—as a matter of fact they make us stronger. When the tears drop and then dry, find strength to conquer.

VOICE

For every thought you have a voice that has been heard and sought. Let that voice speak positivity for the ideas unsought. Let the voice be loud and clear in that inner ear; give your voice life to what matters, louder than you dare.

To be heard you don't have to be the first and you don't have to be the last, you definitely don't listen to that voice that judges your past. Take your time in doing things until you clearly hear what your inner voice is saying. It's that voice that tells you that you are an achiever and not the weaker. It's that voice that tells you that you are an over-comer, it's that voice that tells you to use your wisdom. You just need to listen to the voice that states the grandness you are to become. This is where you have won!

PROUD

When it comes down to people that you care deeply about who made significant accomplishments in life, it's great to tell them you are proud. It's equally important to receive that same acknowledgement for accomplishments.

It's easy to think we are all self-assured and don't need validation from anyone, but in some form we need affirmations from someone. Whether it's a spouse, parent, child, or a friend, we all need someone to help celebrate that accomplishment! We all love to hear I am proud of you; is that not true? So when that special person believes and then achieves, say it out loud that you are proud!

THE PLAN

Can I be where I need to be if you don't allow me? I ask my creator. Am I in your path? I need to go where you lead. I have this plan I envision; it' perfect, it's dear to me, I see my mission, I see then the spirit begin to talk as I listen. A plan is something that human prepares, but a divine order plan is the one I will want you to share that I have prepared. This plan that I prepared was created for you in the womb, so tune into my spirit, tune into my truth, this is where you will hear the plan I have prepared for you.

Only the plan I have for you will be everlasting; it's the gift I give to you that is outstanding! A plan that is preserved, a plan that will change the world. A plan that is not ordinary, a plan that is not rare, a plan beyond this atmosphere. Will you allow me, your creator, to lead you there?

WE MUST ARRIVE

It's not being where we need to go, it's finding where we need to be, that goes for you and me! If we could look in the mirror and see our inner self, we would try to make it pretty as we do our outer self. In order to arrive, you must search your soul to find what makes you whole.

There is a part of us that is not living; just existing. We put on the face powder; the eye shadow to fix our outer self, but when we take the layers off there is nothing left, but us and the mirror. Can we see ourselves? What is missing? There is no completeness. It's time to look ourselves in the face and say, *Self, I am going to find my place of existence and stop hiding behind the shadows' inexistence.*

We must let the world know that we are among the living and we are all extraordinary. We are all born into greatness, and it's time to be alive and make a difference with our existence. It's time to arrive!

I AM

I am perfect in thy entire image. I am grace; I am blessed, through me there is no less. I am the world that completes a full circle that connects from city to city, coast to coast, don't you know? I am the gift that brings the smile. I am the lifter that helps with all the trials. I am the one that heals the lands from miles to miles. I am the motivator that raises you out of your inner graves of self-affliction. I am the one that you must trust as I am the one that turns the dust into life. I am what I am because of the love I have for my creations. I am God, the father of all nations.

THE INNOCENCE

The existence of pure innocence is when you look at your beautiful self; from the moment you enter this world there is love. The love you have is more than life itself. It's precious, it's magical, it emerges from the depth from your soul, the moment you are made whole.

When you give love you find love. You cradle your loved one in your arms, your pure charm, praying, wanting to protect them from harm; knowing that this life is worth living, finding this pure innocence.

Your pure innocence of a new found love as a new baby boy or girl as precious as the gift of a pearl that has come into the world.

I AM IN AWE OF PURE LOVE

You are my gift my blessing. I never knew I could love someone so hard. Your personality reigns in sweet, bubbly, pure respectful, funny smart, honesty. You inspire me in more ways than one. When I look at you, I love to steal your sweet kisses; they are magically and purely delicious. I love to give you hugs; they are my precious moments they are my precious moments shared in pure love. You inspire me to be a better individual. It's unexplainable; I go beyond the heights of my measure to love my truest treasure. Pure love—it's not just love, it's unconditional. Sometimes love can be tainted, but pure love is unadulterated. It's the purest moment when you're in awe of the love.

IS IT SHE, IS IT HE?

Who are we trying to be? Is it he or she? I ask out of the norm, stay tuned into this poem. We undressed and look at ourselves in the mirror; the innocence of the image of nudeness is very pure, but as we dress and look at ourselves in the mirror, the image of ourselves is no longer clears.

As we cover ourselves up and show our exterior, we then are hiding from our inferior. When we put on our layer who are we trying to be, what are we trying to be, is it he, or is it she? Don't choose your outer layers of fashion to try to become the idolatry of the world, but choose your fashion for you to emerge. Emerge not to be he or she, emerge to your true identity.

THE HATERS

Nevertheless you tried to break me. I'm unbreakable. I am not the glass that shattered. I am a person that matters. You continuously try your tricks and schemes with all intent to hurt me by any means. I'm still standing, never falling to my knees; I'm not going to hide my confidence to entertain your insecurities.

You see, I am a person of standards, self-respect, dignity, and that's the difference in me. Your intense dislikes are all on you. Your way of thinking makes you bitter in all things you do. That's your choice, but one day I hope you change your inner voice to stop the self-doubt, because that's the inner root of your hatred, your bigotry, your negativity. Find your sense of self-love, and then you will find yourself opening up from hatred and rise above.

CRITICS

Our critics may make you feel our work may be unworthy, un-accomplished, lacking depth, but it also could be honorable. You can't let praise or criticism get to you. It's a weakness to get caught in either one. You have to let your heart speak to your work and choose not to let critics determine your self-worth. There is no effort without error, but you know your work is from your blood, sweat, and tears. You are at your best knowing in the end your efforts are your triumphs and the words from your timid souls who know neither victory nor defeat.

FEAR

What's in our voice that I hear? Is it fear? Do you not want the freedom to live for the gifts the creator gives? Our creator does not accept fear or the concept of Forever Rejection. He accepts faith, meaning Forever Always in the Helm. The helms of his will, the helm of I can, the helm of his ordained plan, the helm of his purpose for you.

Fear is not a part of your life as an objective; don't let fear cause you to be forever in rejection! What will you become when you live in fear, subjecting yourself to self-doubts always without!

IMPOSSIBLE TO POSSIBLE

Why are we here? I dare to have dreams and goals to master. We're supposed to sit and stare out of broken glasses that are shattered—that's our dream, a pale illusion, shattered by obstacles, making them impossible to conquer. Out lack of discipline, seems unpleasant, why this total hesitance? Lack of discipline consumes our drive-keeping us from advocating for ourselves to strive.

Pick up them broken glasses and make that abstract view clear, you have a dream inside of you to share! Turn them obstacles into possible, everything else will follow. Don't run after money, people, fame, or success, not the success that is measured by money, but the success of knowledge, action, and excellence. Focus in on turning those impossibilities into possibilities and those possibilities into realties.

THE SATURDAY GLOW

Wake up, America, it's the day to play, find your Disney with your children or yourself, explore, be creative, bash into the sunshine of this day, be fierce like the wind, and let the cares just blow away with it.

If you have to work, it's not for the entire day or night. When it's time for you to get off, get that boost of energy and enjoy the sight.

If it rains, don't complain; watch the rain flow against the window pane. Let it calm and soothe your inner glow, let it bring you inner peace as the rain pours; let it cleanse your soul.

Experiment no matter how the weather is or if duties call, don't let it steal your joy. Find your happy dance, take a chance on yourself. You may discover your hidden talents. Besides, it's Saturday, the best day of the week to sleep, to dress, to mess, to create, to date, to have fun in the sun, or to do chores if the rain pours. Whatever you choose to do let Saturday be your day to play and explore!

SERENE SUNDAY

It's a new day in America, it's the day of the week that's named after the sun that brings forth light as Jesus is the light. It's the day to reflect, to prepare, and partake with family that is near. Sunday feels like calmness. It's a day of prominence, importance, adherence, a day of beliefs, a day of peace.

Sundays are meant for comfort, solace, contentment, to be in the moment and to be released of negativity and resentments. Be of good encouragement and to be in the moment of solitude and of good gratitude.

Sundays are joyous, free from the nonsense noise, when there are moments of peace in your poise. You take a stroll for a blissful escape, the time is slow, no rush, free to enjoy the sun's glow; it's so surreal in dreamscape.

Sundays are sports, where you get to cheer and represent your team in your favorite sports gear. This is the team you love, hoping they win and rise above. As Sunday winds down and you prepare for the next day, you reflect on what a good day is Sunday!

GRIEF

I must say to you, grief is borne of loneliness, that pain of emptiness is everlasting. Grief has nowhere to go, it resides in you until you release the tears and allow them flow. Grief is a life long journey that we cope with and seek God for grace and mercy.

REMEMBRANCE

We shall not forget the love, the life of the loved ones we lost, that we feel no pain of guilt or remorse. Now, when alone with your thoughts, one reflects on a moment that you love the most; the conversations, the touch, the laugh, or the boast. Forever in your heart, with this connection you will never be apart.

THE ANGELS

You get an inkling something that is about to happen. How is it going to happen? It's a question of the unknown, and you try to figure it out on your own; you start to look around, but there is no one to be found. You feel your heart, or the problem you've been struggling with, is no longer a worry. You feel your heart—you get a sense of relief, then peace, then your Spirit brings to you remembrance. Look toward heaven! There is a beautiful array on display; and your heavenly angels watch over you every step of the way.

THE MASTERPIECE

My dad, my guiding force, there was nothing we longed for. He instilled in us to get our education. We were blessed by him and he gave us the motivation; he was our inspiration. The masterpiece—our father—admirable and most of all lovable. A piece in our heart is missing, but having him as our father was such a blessing. Rest on, our father in heaven. He was truly a masterpiece in his children's eyes, giving us his all, standing tall, making sure we never fall, loving us no matter what, blessing us with his presence and his fatherly grace.

MIRACLE

You can see it; you can feel it from within, that extraordinary experience of the unknown, a force, a transforming moment. A wow factor—it's pure, it cures, it reassures, out of difficulties comes miracles, the barrier blocks dissolve. I am in awe of the gift of a miracle.

SICK AND TIRED

You see, I was a fence, locked in, taking all this nonsense. I'm out of here, not walking in fear, not shedding another tear, not listening to a liar—you see when you are sick and tired, you are just sick and tired. I am tired of this mess, got me stressing, thinking I am nothing but less, but now I must confess I am the best. I'm going to pull off my pretty dress, step in my stilettos, and walk in confidence, not look back in hesitance, but look for to distance.

JOURNEY

How clear the moon shines! I lie beneath, and by the guidance of light, stars are twinkling at me. Tomorrow wake, but dream tonight. In my dreams I open my heart and let it speak and all the powerlessness of my inner mind be revealed. I feel fear I feel starting a new journey, love, parenthood—all scary but fulfilling. It's the flesh in us that keeps us dreaming by the darkness of the moon, but it's the spirit in us that awakens us from our dreams, by the sun's brightness, and opens my heart to the power in me to begin this new journey.

THE EXPERIENCE

It's unbelievable, it's magical, it's powerful, it lifts boundaries, it's beyond amazing, and it's living. What's life without experience? It's nothing! Let experience be your life's lesson; learn, grow, create, dare to be scared, to be open, to be more, remove fear, don't be afraid. Let your experiences be beyond what your mind can measure, let it be an experience you can treasure.

POWER

I must insist you let me tell you what power is. I own me. I contend with my own destiny. I'm not inferior to your skin tone. I'm rising to fulfill by destiny. I'm taking charge of the most significant inner part: my thoughts, my heart. Only positive energy—that is my new body language, that is what I intend to manage. Prepare yourself, every minute of the hour, to declare a positive power.

MARRIAGE

Brides, before you make that choice to walk down the aisle to state your vows, before you make the change in your lifestyle, embark on these words of this poem. Grooms before you, make that choice to stand at the altar and vow to your bride, embark on these words in this poem as a guide.

Marriage is a commitment that requires nurturing for growth; there's true meaning behind this sacred oath. Marriage is the story of two individuals that came together as partners in life; full of plots and series of causes and effects that could cause strife, but with work it can suffice. Marriage is loyalty, honesty, trust, takes diligence and respect. It's the commitment between two that you vow to project. Marriage is passion, compassion, affectionate, purity, and sex. These marital elements are pertinent essentials. Marriage is patience, gentleness, kindness, thoughtfulness, and forgiveness. Its all these qualities compiled that make marriages meaningful and worthwhile.

In marriage let there be love as love bears all things, hopes believes all things, endures all things. Let all you do in in love.

SEXUALITY

Sexuality with so many different forms exists in this world, some we don't know as boy or girl. It's the most uncomfortable talk that many have in America. I know many communities avoid recognizing some forms of sexuality they see as acceptable. They have their beliefs and values with distinguished ways of thinking with their influential stature.

Sexuality is fluid; everyone's sexual preference is unique and inimitable. Sexuality is described in so many different categories; whether you are heterosexual, homosexual, bisexual, queer, or asexual, it's your story.

Sexuality is your freedom, it's your passion, it's what you have come to know about yourself that's everlasting.

Sexuality is your business, and with your sexuality it comes from within. When you have come in to your own and believe this is your truth, that's how you win within.

Your sexuality is your truth! Stop hiding that part of yourself from the most important person and that is you!

A MAN'S WORLD INSIDE OF HERS (HUSBAND AND WIFE)

He tells her no when she asks. It strokes his ego, but deep down he wants to be her hero. He smiles because of her heavenly glow. He aims to please her every desire; it's the love she gives him that he admires. He dreams to meet her every need, to fulfill all her fantasies. He has peace when she is calm; he sleeps with comfort when she's in his arms. That's the protective nature in him, to be the lover, the friend, the gentlemen, and the man until the end.

His gentlemanlike qualities appear. There's a stare enlightened by the mood in the air. The tone he speaks brings forth a quiver, which makes her shiver. The essence of smooth, charm, and charisma, the gentlemen that he was raised to be! That's a man that knows how to treat his lady!

THE LYRIC OF LOVE

I found my beauty in a place of music and sound, full of sweet tones that were profound. In the midst of it all there was a gentleman clothed like the nature of fall; his beauty stood so tall, the smile bold as a fiery moon, made my blood burn and swoon.

He graces my presence with open hands and asks, "Shall we dance?" There are lyrics that play accordingly in my mind as we dance. The first lyric, he holds me close as we listen with his gentleman like touch. The second lyric of pleasure my soul said in me, This *is so marvelous*..I felt he could do no harm. The third lyric is a delight as he kisses me with soft laughter and in a smooth tone he whispered, "Good night," and I held him so tight.

LOVE

Love shows up, it doesn't hide. Love brings you a sense of pride. Love is doing the simple things—a simple call or text to do a wellness check. Love keeps you committed; it's that mutual bond that keeps you connected. Love is that obscure feeling that reveals itself through the eyes. Love is a special touch that exudes happiness; love is a gift that allows you to experience something magnificent.

Love builds healthy relationships, friendships, and kinships that are built to last when you nourish it. Love will shine and can't be dimmed; love is what the world needs, it's enthusiasm. Love is the most affectionate emotion you can feel, it's appealing, it's receiving, being loved is amazing! Love conquers all things bad, even when the world is mad; when you have love you are glad!

Love feeds your soul with truth and comfort; love does not cause harm or anyone to suffer. Love brings a deep connection that's far beyond superficial; being loved is unconditional. Love is connection, love is affection, and love is a champion that goes hard for their companion. Love is having someone's best interest, and love is trust. Love is love that comes from within, and long as we live, there will be love that will never end.

MENTAL HEALTH TRUTHS

Unemployment rates rises, the deaths of COVID-19, devastating gun violence—what are we to do, we can't live in silence! Opening up about mental health issues is really hard, but it has to be done, especially if you feel that your mental stability is your number one job.

The 911 calls hurt us all when tragedies have taken place in neighborhoods, malls, and even the school halls. This type of realization—owning your truth about your mental health issues—can help save lives as America doesn't have to see another person die. There is no doubt that you should reach out for professional help and inform someone about any mental health struggles. This is a lifesaving tip to help avoid further troubles.

PROBLEM RELATIONSHIPS

Let's talk the truth to ourselves when we deal with relationships. I tell you what; that boyfriend, girlfriend, wife, husband, or partner is the hardest to conquer. We tend to hide from the truth when we don't want to be bothered.

A lot of neglected issues tend to get swept under the rug, because people don't want to deal with the underlying issues that could be causing the friction, don't want to expose what you don't want dug.

There are going to be growing pains in your relationship with your significant other. How can you keep hiding in a relationship and continue to suffer?

Can you be honest with your significant other when you have experienced growth and they are not on the same growing path you are on? When you have outgrown them!

Hanging on to something that is not there—it makes you well aware! This is a waste of time when there's so much strife! You cannot have a one-way love; that would make it impossible to hug!

You may work hard to ignore the problem, but you are going to experience unwanted tension from your partner.

You are going to experience your share of unwanted aches, which make you wonder where they are coming from, feeling numb because you don't know how you are going to over-come.

You are going to be off- balance in all areas of your life until you reveal the truth and begin to thrive. Either you or your significant other will need counseling or you will have to come to the conclusion—this relationship is dying.

When you don't come to your truth, one or the other is going to have an entanglement and often one is left in detriment! There are signs that will be revealed through their actions as there will be no more satisfaction!

Life is too valuable. Find your happiness and your truth. Let that toxic lie go and find your happiness in you.

I believe you have to let your significant other know something is not right in the relationship, or you will be one miserable person just drowning in life like a sinking ship!

Another aspect of relationship truths: Can you be honest if you are not attracted to your significant other anymore? When you first met them they were well fit; now there's no attraction even a little bit.

As the years progressed, your significant other gained weight by eating with no self-care. This revelation might hurt self-esteem here.

You have to be careful with your words, because you are going to be revealing some uncomfortable information that doesn't want to be heard.

When releasing this truth I hope your significant other can stand to hear this type of information and begin to do some self-improvement and have a positive transformation.

What about if you have fallen out of love with them? To find your truth with this question will come from your soul, but this revelation has to be told.

If you don't feel empathy for your partner and don't have a desire to explore new things, then it's time to give back the wedding ring!

When you don't care about the time or distance separating you two, you will find yourself in space becoming a wanderer!

It's time to move on when you don't want to experience physical intimacy; that's not a love of authenticity!

You must tune into your heart and your inner wisdom and remember that whatever you are feeling is an indication of whether what you are thinking and believing is line with your true self. Challenging your current beliefs and getting back to your true beliefs is a journey of self-care.

What if your significant other is belittling you and physically abusing you? Please don't make excuses for they are revealing their true nature. Run, because this is pure hatred!

More likely their true self knows nothing else but to abuse and to use! Get out and leave because this person will not change—this person is easily set off and lives in rage!

Leave in order to save your life, and if there are children involved, leave to save their lives and also leave to save the abuser's life. The best way to end an abusive relationship is always to leave and be free! Trust yourself, and trust the process through problem relationships.

WHEN YOU TRY NOT TO CARE

Sometimes you have the moment in your life when you stop trying to care because everything is so hideous, or most things feel perfidious and people are so surreptitious.

They just keep things undercover and just do wrong to others. You have these people that are so loquacious and their stubborn ways are so tumultuous—these people are so impetuous.

You can be the one that is obedient, but then there are the disobedient that seem to have everything go their way, and it just leaves you in dismay. This is not okay. Your *okays* have to turn into *This is not my way*; your heart is built different, you have a heart of benevolence. When you care, your ways of thinking become cognizant. You are tuned in to the knowledge and awareness of how your words affect someone, so you learn to be conscientious about everyone's feelings.

You have the feeling of *I need to care when I try not to care.* You have to tune into your reasoning, and your reasoning will lead you to a magnanimous season of forgiving and living beyond those *I don't care* moments, turning them into remnants. No one will get away with hurting people, so when you have that *I don't care* attitude, seek gratitude that one day, for those that did the wrong, karma will come and it won't take long.

THE VOICE OF A CHILD

Do we matter, with our smiles and giggles and laughter? Our schools are so neglected, and we are not being protected. We are not safe to run freely in our playgrounds. Instead we scream from the loose bullets of gun sounds. Every day is a concern of gun violence as we gather to learn and wonder. Do they care for us? Every day we hope our screams are not of fear, but of laughter and sounds of good cheer; the cheers of playful moments that give us enjoyment.

Every boy and every girl deserve the chance to amaze this world. As Whitney Houston sang, I believe our children are the future; our children deserve to be cared for and nurtured and not in danger of losing their young life through gun violence and murder.

Representatives, our children deserve better—and not the cliché sayings of our thoughts and prayers, but gun laws being passed, so our children can stop being murdered in the masses. Our dear country that we so loved, our children want a way of living of how things once were, where they can go to school to learn, to play, and to feel safe and to return home where they are embrace.

FRIENDSHIPS

Friendship is clearly necessary and splendid, it's not a relationship you take for granted. Friendships are a connected feeling of goodwill between two or more people; its growth continues when you feel you are equal.

Friendship is unique where both people derive benefit from each other, when you are drawn together for comfort and laughter.

Friendship is goodness, where you admire the goodness, it's the conversations shared that bring forth insightfulness. Goodness is an enduring quality, so friendships based on goodness tend to be long lasting, and the experiences shared are enchanting.

Friendship encompasses two people like a safe cocoon. Friendships are rare and take time to develop, but at its best friendship can withstand any test.

Friendship is the act of loving rather than the act of being loved; friendship is a gift from above.

Friendship is an essential component of the good life, and the value of friendship is having and enjoying life.

Friendships can have a positive effect on your life and your health. When you have a positive friendship with those that genuinely care, this friendship will last until death.

HIGH NOTES OF POETRY

First Lyric: *High* represents the highest extent, the grandest, the intensity. High is greater than normal, high is phenomenal, and high is favorable, notable, and honorable. High is admirable, successful, your happy place, high is grace. High is the state of elation, high is state of exhilaration.

Second Lyric: *Notes* signify importance; notes are a defining pitch that gives you goose bumps during a grand performance. Notes give attention; it's a sentiment that resonates through our senses that bring forth happiness. Notes bring connection as they transcend into our emotions leaving you with intensification.

High Notes of Poetry represents these lyrics with all my heartfelt emotions and values that I hoped to have a lasting impact on someone life. The words authentically embody every aspect of my being. *High Notes* encourages confidence, displays love, and gives you strength to persevere, to turn impossible to possible, to have strength to embrace fear. *High Notes* is my voice!

QUOTES FOR DAILY LIFE

Don't let quickness stop you from your greatness.
If I fail or if I succeed, my works will count indeed.
All creativity is made in beauty by the creator.
When in doubt, opt out.
Seek peace in your decision-making; peace helps calm the hesitation.
Be free, forever ready for every excursion.
Those who take chances make advances.
All opportunities are not great opportunities.
It's best to prepare for an opportunity than to have an opportunity and not be prepared.

ABOUT THE AUTHOR

Ellen Brown Harrison is a professional, an advocate, a wife, a mother, and so much more. She has won awards through her employers, volunteer to aid in the lives of resource-insecure members of her community. Ellen is a member of an organization that promotes health and wellness education for teen girls. Ellen also volunteers with an organization through Public Education Outreach that help promote young students interest in STEM careers.

Ellen's volunteer work remains boundlessly optimistic and backed by faith. Poetry writing became a source of strength to help cope with the death of her father.

She was born and raised in Allendale, South Carolina. Today, she lives in Aiken SC, with her supportive husband of 28 years and their daughter.

Author Ellen Harrison releases her first poetry collection that soothes the soul, encourages empowerment, and reveals the inner strength of every reader.